Messages from the Bees

Messages from the Bees

New Poems
Robin Winckel-Mellish

modjaji books

PREVIOUS PUBLICATIONS

POETRY
A Lioness at my Heels

First published in 2017 by Modjaji Books
© Robin Winckel-Mellish 2017
ISBN 978-1-928215-35-6

Cover image by Fiona Moodie
Design and typesetting by Louise Topping
Printed and bound by Digital Action

For Charlie

CONTENTS

Three

One

Homing Pigeons

A whirring, then gone in a flash.
In the silver-flecked sky,
tails glint in the sun.
Wheeling in unison,
pigeons flash a fleeting cloud
across a blue-scraped horizon.

What makes them hurry home?
Does the speed of their flying
bring news to us,
their compass-like alignments
ensuring a mad sky-scramble
nothing can stop?

Our own anagrams of flight
are a place where the loved one lives,
as magnets in the top of a pigeon's beak,
and in the groin, neat and small,
that ancient impulse, to dart
and peak and bring us home.

Caracal

I had walked there for years, head down
and checking for cat-paw tracks,
now at last alive as I stand
and watch you move,

cat body hidden by bush,
head facing the dunes,
unaware, red tail brushing the sand,
forward, backward, forward, backward.

It gives you away, late afternoon light
catching rust on an open patch,
the minutes passing until suddenly
you turn tufted ears and, surprised,

draw back tense lips, your wild eyes
for one second penetrating mine
before you leap and turn
and vanish in a flash.

We have weekend guests at the house,
and a past lover, not seen in decades.
We sidestep with care, talk small
and brush sand over all our tracks.

Messages from the Bees

Every sound has a story.
Regular breath, a slow heartbeat,
the bubbling of morning porridge,
leaves that in a trembling breeze

drift and rustle on frozen ground,
rainwater laughing down
the gutters after a sudden storm
has drifted farther on.

In an African garden I found
a deep hole where you can hear
the humming of the earth,
making us thrill in these bodies

where we find ourselves,
your breath echoing in my ear
and carrying into me
messages from the bees.

The Migrant

swoops down,
as if he owns my house,
and wants me away.
Bags in hand, I've arrived
after a long-haul flight
to find a feathered intruder.
Suddenly, he perches close by,
head and nape slate blue,
crown slightly rufous,
eyes dark brown, bill
pinkish around the nostrils,
maize legs grasping
the high bar of my pergola.
Now I understand –
the potted plant on my terrace
has become his larder.
Then he's off on a breeze,
a swift, dark shape in sky,
while flies have gathered
on the fleshy leaves of an aloe.
At dusk I return to find
his sharp beak tearing in-
to the meat of a mouse.
In the mirror I must revise
who I thought I was.

The Kestrels

come back in September,
this year nesting in the owl box.
Their high view overlooks
a spring wilderness, the distant
shocking yellow canola fields,
a grey smudge of mountains.

Kik-ki-ki … our noisy visitors
have arrived early with their shrill
shrieks echoing around me
as I watch them swoop and hover,
then deliver another mouse
to their brand new wooden nest.

They're so much busier than me,
their relentless droppings of mice
exhausting. I can only relax
on my verandah, coffee in hand,
raise a cup as if toasting them.
Seen all, done all – your turn.

The Wind in Ten Movements

I
Among the sea and scrub
the cantabile movement
of the wind sings out
to an unpeopled world.

II
The fiery-necked nightjar rings
in with his plaintive whistle,
good lord deliver us as he
rides in the palm of the wind.

III
Our breath is the wind
uneven, then elevated;
it gropes, *a ritornello*,
silky and untouched.

IV
The little white gate
bangs in moonlight,
my torched hand shuts
the sharp sound.

V
The lonely curtain flaps
and snaps. Boats
moving south line up.
I set sail in my house.

VI
An owl standing still
on the tin roof is braced
on the shadow of a song:
three hours until daybreak.

VII
Rain hammers, the sea drums,
little rivers on the track outside;
whistling wind scuttles
round the corners of the walls.

VIII
Wheat fields in the distance are
electric in the light, the wind
lets loose its wild orchestra;
a madman bangs the doors.

IX
At 6am, the wind suddenly
lifts, a strange sucking sound;
a scorpion dances in the bedclothes,
its fighting pincers up.

X
A concord of night sounds;
the ocean bed lies ruffled;
snow horses pile up in
regular, symphonic waves.

Earth Shades in Morning

I'm thinking about how
the other people
(Bushmen to be precise)
live off necessity
and how maidens
(and even married women)
lift their skirts and run away,
how women court men
and men court women,
how they sit together
with tangled legs.

Everything is clear
this early morning:
the landscape, burnt bark,
dried river beds
as cracked capillaries,
a cinnamon rust in the sky.
I'm dressed in shades
of tortoiseshell and oxblood,
the ashen taste of smoke
on my tongue.

Fingertips

A commotion in sludge-thick rain.
Gut string of croaks, sky pitched:
I'm here, here, I'm over here,
and the distant response:

Come get me, get me, get me.
All night an alarm clock
shrieks a season. I dream
of him, noisy as a bull, tiger-

striped, warty, all puffed up
and anxious to jump a female.
Then the morning sun reveals
how small he actually is:

tiny as a thumbnail, nestling
wet in my hand, webbed feet
and a thrumming frog heart beating
it's me, it's me, it's me.

The Poet Who Talks to Birds

She steps out from the rocking cable car,
having come for the flat sandstone rocks
and a far view: a cudgel-shaped island

and, further on, an invisible South Pole,
the city in miniature, a swarm below.
In front, a gregarious young starling

lands on a rock, iridescent in the sun,
its sooty head tilted sideways, perplexed
by the poet's mimicked whistle.

He twitters a showy riff in return,
one chirped stanza after another.
Did he discover rhyme in the rhythm

of his whistle? There is little distance
between them, the poet whistling back,
melding with the bird's line of song.

The Nun Who Saves Saplings

All summer long she keeps
a rendezvous with the orchard,
arriving to walk alone
in the gloaming under plum trees,
in the neat rows on the hill,
their fruit as round as the sky,
the cropped meadow grass
beneath her feet a stubby carpet
as far as the deep forest
where a growing together
of wilderness stops others
from entering there.

Late after a long hour's chanting
she hurries to reach where
the mower can't cut,
where the high grass hides
saplings of oak and beech,
chestnut and pine, where
she kneels to carefully dig,
laying them in her basket
before walking back in prayer
to plant them in terracotta.
After a year, she will return
to the forest to replant them,
when they are strong.

Her hands are stained with joy.

Nightlife

1

It's midnight. Just below the dunes
a fox barks farther down the street,
although all trees around are bare,
bright burning lights within the house
are flickerings of nightly cheer.

2

The moon slides slowly down its arc,
goodbyes are said, the night goes quiet;
the kitchen fire has burned down,
casts shadows as dreams on the walls,
the answering vixen's yips are shrill.

3

The thin, pale light is watery,
she stands and watches from the window.
Warm blooded, furtive and hungry,
the vixen tiptoes silently out
of the gardens, back into the woods.

All Creatures

A wasp-like winged insect
has been dragging a spider
back and forth on the warm
cement floor of the terrace.

It seems content to stay close
to the door, pushing and pulling
in little circles, worrying over
the hairy mass of spider legs.

A shrew ran in from the dark,
crisscrossed the room, before
diving into my shopping bags.
I had to send him onwards.

The resident cobra tried to climb
a shadow on the wall, failing
and falling back to the floor,
again and again, only vanishing

when out I walk with my pen and paper
to sit and struggle. On this morning,
only the rushing, folding sea
seems confident of its rhythms.

The Teachings of the Ants

When a blue sea laps our doorstep,
when rain swells dizzy waters,
when wind blows off the heads of trees
and a poker heat burns and burns our gardens
until they are black, when we
hunger all day for the food we knew

will we cry out to the ants somewhere below,
so comfortable in their labyrinths,
the grass-cutting ants constructing turrets
by kneading balls of clay in their jaws,
building, building, and steadily making
their air-conditioned nests

with level paths to connect
chamber to chamber, the ancient ants,
around a hundred million years.
When it all goes wrong, will we
honour their gods, look down and know
we've so much more to learn,

knowing then they will not miss us?

Organic

We are, it seems, above the tortuous summer,
fire-blackened trees down to the vineyard.

Up here, gardener Livingstone has picked
the plums and pomegranates that cling on.

Fluffy eucalyptus blooms give off
their heady, gum-tingling smell

in the stillness of the vegetable garden
where we are already thinking of winter,

digging and clearing for the next season
of marigolds, tomatoes, straw and seedlings,

humus and mulching, rocket for salads.
The porcupine trap on the narrow side

of the bed remains resolutely empty.
Compost lies a heap, and the wormery

spills loose soil. At the bottom of the hill
the dead are all loyal to the earth.

Owls at Christmas

I walked beside your house to feel
the chill of Christmas eve,
the damp that's blown in over dunes,
the soft and blurring fur of mist
that clings to rhododendrons,
the dark street lit by strings of candles
orchestrated by the breeze.

Tired of an over-stuffed house
and the colour red, I gasped
at all the echoing sounds of owls
perched in your garden's leafless tree,
their hoots and answers followed by
a range of strange and cat-like squawks
that marked their flight in fading light
away to darkened, empty forest.

Two

Aubade

He arrived just before sunrise,
flushed little body, scrawny legs;
unlike the late flickering of spring,
on time, his little hands curled

like tiny leaves, a small Buddha,
eyes hardly open, peaceful,
knowing only suck, his small head
resting on her radiant breast.

The dawn struck pink through
narrow chinks in the curtains,
the night broken, breathing light
into a world still taking shape.

Next door, the young inside
the Amsterdam 'wonder lounge'
are milling round, working at ways
to spend more time out of their heads,

not imagining that like us,
they'll not live forever.

Mapping Our Universe

I measure your face, a stream
of falling stars as we butterfly swim
the white wave of the small bed,

bodies adrift skyways, cutting
this night out of the universe
to explore our light and shadow

the world rushing away from us.
We have nothing to fear from each other,
not the unexplored dark spaces,

the shores of backs and shoulders,
lunar forests, luminous and alive,
the Mappa Mundi of circles and codes,

the language of our dents and curves
as we are lit by the rising sun,
dying into each other, becoming one.

A Man, His Dog and His Lover

Reverse roles. The lover is the dog, the dog is the lover. The lover waits at home. It is growing dark, the hills are dim in distance. She has not yet been fed. On the other side of the city a man leaves a dog in a four-poster bed and goes home. The dog shivers wearing only a small fur collar. It is September and already a chill has set in. The dog is barking a goodbye from the wrought iron balcony. It does not want him to leave. It goes back into the room decorated with crystal droplets and pink roses. It howls. There are lights on all over the city. Soft music plays from a radio. The dog cannot understand how the man could leave, when he could so easily have stayed. Yet the man is whistling quietly and is happy. He is on his way home to feed his lover.

Losing Face

He'd lost his face,
I didn't recognize him,
heavier now, his body
corralled in puttied flesh,
eyes shadowed with time.
In a family photo, I retrace
those features back through
the oceans of adulthood,
anchoring driftwood and gulls,
winds whipped to a frenzy,
ghosts stalking the smells of salt,
sun lotion; a tidal wave
churning our adolescence.
Our dolphin bodies were slender.
I touch my eyes, my forehead.
My skin has lain against
the earth, under the sun.
Would you know me?

The Monkey Jumps Down

The stage is dimmed and the player performs
with hands like a pair of miniature athletes
running up and loping down the piano.

His right foot treads and treads the pedal
while the left is tapping a jamboree.
He's at ease, his fingers moving effortlessly,

they are used to living their lives apart.
He is asked to play old numbers, asked to sing
what he's never known or found or thought.

His pet monkey sits on top of the piano,
tries to steal the cherry from someone's cocktail;
in jungle heat beyond the windows, the city swings.

When the song ends, the crowd roars its approval,
the monkey jumps down, knocking over the glass
from which cherry and cocktail are missing.

Our Alignment

I shall walk from
lighthouse to lighthouse,
from Danger Point
to Pearly Beach,
across the long
open stretch where
two oceans meet,
stopping to remember:
The Barry's,
Star of the Isles,
Trevelyn and
The Lord Hawkesbury –
so many ships
wrecked and rusting.
I will learn
the impossible language
of birds and whales,
dig Bushman middens
to find signs
of your presence,
hoping to meet
your warm shadow
in the light
on the water,
its beam shining
full circle.

Found Letter

The Cederberg Mountains are bathed in deep blue;
in each curve of shape, I recall your presence,
in the bodies of contour, each incline is you.

Ripe for the sickle, you cut me right through,
overwhelmed by a sense of deepening sentience.
In the bodies of contour, each incline is you.

The tongue of the moon in the morning dew
held me, excited by your effervescence.
The Cederberg Mountains are bathed in deep blue.

The wrinkled old shirt you slowly outgrew
I keep smoothing out for remembrance.
In the bodies of contour, each incline is you.

Will I never forget the night that you flew,
I'm still filled with a sense of your essence;
the Cederberg Mountains are bathed in deep blue.

In letters I thought lost, again I have found you,
elliptical lines brimful with your presence.
The Cederberg Mountains are bathed in deep blue.
In the bodies of contour, each incline is you.

Please Play the Old Piano

The snow never came this year,
so now let from your fingers flow
fresh, loud and soft music
as doves come back to nest
in the wisteria's gardens of purple.

The snow didn't come this year,
so let come from your fingers
unstoppable sounds
for the change of season,
the shuffling of wings.

The snow stayed away this year,
so let flow from your piano
urgent explosions
to bring us alive, luminous and bare,
going into a glowing new season.

Postcard from Another Era

Faces angled to almost kiss
scaly feet poised as tortoise oars,
the artist has them on a panel,

oil on paper, my words
on the back, sweet and pretty
as I poke the shell of memory.

Ik heb je lief
in neat blue words, a few
lines on an anniversary.

Scales locked, earth touching
on torn paper, the African slow ones
click a forgotten past into focus.

The End of the World

It can only be the end of the world, as you move forward

ARTHUR RIMBAUD

I ran along the cliffs,
the wind buffeting against me,
seeing the sea suck
into itself, shocked fish
looking out from the waves.

Gulls had taken shelter
in the mouth of a cave,
a tortoise marched, naked
in the burning bush, the sky
had turned a dark plumbago.

I lay on the red rocks,
hair flaring and teeth rattling,
exhilarated by the thought
of lying down with the world,
witnessing its final passion.

Dilemmas

They were there for days,
a clump of people on a rock
the sea sparkling with summer,
their makeshift home littered
all around: bright blankets, fires,
clothing and cooking utensils.

From my chair in the house
I could see them waiting,
smell the wood smoke drifting
from open fires, witness their
uncertain grooming, anxious talking,
clean people watching from afar.

Further down the line, an anthill
of dark men exploded into life
as they swarmed across the tarmac,
following moving trucks, forcing
doors open
          while in Africa

herds of black-maned wildebeest agonised
over whether or not to cross water
to the promise of the other side.
Rain clouds built in the distance,
a rich, sweet earth-smell rising
through the layered heat of the day.

The Meaning of Deserved

Go down to the rubbish dump,
you'll be greeted by wolf-eyed men,
lame dogs, bulldozers flattening
an African mountain of stench,
plastic blowing onto a barbed fence.
They'll say hello, shamelessly take
your black bag and begin to unpack
it right in front of you. A man's
got to do what a man's got to do,
says the dreadlocked man with
the body of a girl, doing time
in the hell hole bordering
my paradise. And us?
What else is there to do
when the world decides for you,
falling into a thorny unknown?
Now pink straws of a dawn show
as diluted blood on a cleared horizon,
our new day seemingly deserved.
I told this to the tree snake that
spent the winter in the woodshed,
just a slither of colour
in the meshing of its body,
most of it hidden in the eaves,
protected and warm, its head
looking down, its forked tongue
busily testing, its motionless stare
hungry for the food of Spring.

Hy Was 'n Goeie Man

He knew them all by name:
Elsie at the petrol pump,
Yvonne at the laundry,
Rowena from the farm stall,
the old sick man and his dog
at the rubbish dump,
brought them all the nylon clogs
from far-off Holland
they wore to Sunday service.

We'd been going there
for a decade, the ugly
little seaside town.
And now I do the chores.
They want to know
how I could have left him
in such a cold country.
Hy was 'n goeie man,
ons sal hom mis.

The Rain at Bodhi Khaya

The sound of rain is different here,
it beats just like a small bird's wings
and resonates in the echoing space
between the ceiling made of reeds

and pushed-together narrow beds
in which we burrow to find the centre
of the folding day, with dusk and night
entwined in delicate layers of light.

The season of cold is passing, although
the milkwood remains an intricate work
rendered in ink, the trees half-dormant,
quietly stirring in the late winter glow.

Though tired, we've shaken off the yoke,
are reinventing love, create a new sense
of belonging as serenity flows from a place
beyond the past to the quiet grace of now.

Our silence lies in patience acquired,
our eyes the way we touch and sense,
the distance between us a silvered thread,
the future's amulet our recompense.

Etchings in Dust

This is the house we always had,
a box of matches, a pile of wood,
wild olives from the dune forest.
No garden, though the ericas
and red disas blow and blur
before the pale glow of saltmarshes.

Some evenings the local mongoose
slips by in the yellow, sea-blue light,
with little ears and a dark tail tip,
his claw prints etched in dust,
and traces everywhere of that
'whatever it is' that never fades –
a kind voice like the noise of water.

Grieving with Elephants

As if gates have opened
friends flood in
with flowers and fruit,
whispering in the hot room.

I'd rather the plain elephants
and a simple landscape –
a quiet sorrow in a world
rich with nothing.

They would surround me gently,
reach out with swaying trunks
their size embodying sorrow,
as they stand and dust themselves,

their low rumblings an orison.
Moving off, their powdered ears
would flap like the wings of seraphim –
dream vision of a temporal union.

Sleeping with Morpheus

Side by side we find ourselves
in our unspeakable world,
the curve of a chair
draped with your night shirt,
your bedside table filled with opiates,
the room a small cave
tightly holding your pain.
Heavy curtains hold
an inner garden, the rise
and fall of each other's dreams,
the high tree outside
drenched with night.
Our touching limbs
have lulled the demons,
dream messenger Morpheus
has scattered his poppy seeds,
while your sleeping face
and frail, winged back
are all that is.

Lovebirds at the Pain Clinic

He nuzzles up to her as she bends
to him in his wheelchair.

Her little strokes and twitters
come into focus from behind

the coffee machine as they move
in time to join the lengthening line,

her centred, focused hands and feet,
his naked head and sallow cheeks.

She pushes at the weightless chair
with dedicated tenderness,

their small ship nosing at the quay,
all the others in the room

no more than shadows in their light,
circling, silent or murmuring,

waiting on the shore for relief.

Intimate

The two of us lying there,
my young hands touching
ebony, a cat licking
and loose as a cheetah
on the run, I was
unfurled sail,
speechless as the sea,
beyond control, breath
stirring the outermost
layer of pearl, nerve endings
thin as a peel of fruit,
the husk of closeness
so delicate it trilled.
Now, old hands
feel out the ghosts
of intimacy, the soft
pelt of animal curled
around inner stone,
as bones eaten clean,
ivory glistening
in the warm shadow
of tenderness.

Carrying a King

Candles burn, curtains are half-drawn,
the morning has ended as the rest
of a day opens, bedroom doors
a gateway to the freshness of garden:
hedges quiet, trees motionless,
branched, saluting, the stretch of grass
seeming to lead to some great place.

Like a home birth, whispered his sister.
His face lit up, not a dark alley
but an ending that seemed a beginning.
Like a starfish back in water he relaxed
and let go, allowing us to lift him high,
step by step carrying him out.

The Home Bringing

We wondered, months later,
whether we'd done right by him,
by not moving him out
through a hole in the wall
of the house so he wouldn't
remember the way back;
not taking the zigzag path
to the burial site, throwing
sharp thorns on the way
so that he wouldn't become
a wandering ghost.
None of this had we done,
no ash smeared on the windows,
the photographs not turned,
how would he have received
a new body to enable him
to move about his world?
Left behind, we didn't forget
the world's a light and living place,
knew he'd be happy to
lightfoot the journey,
so we feasted and sang,
remembering the way
the passage of time
had worked on him,
and declared our faith
in the world of the perishable,
the great wound staining us all,
the slain ox bringing him
back home to his family,

and we pressed our lips
into the earth, weighted
our voices with silence,
grasped the past's
transcendent dust.

Three

When the Land Becomes the Moon

The Bushwoman wakes,
her buttocks slack and shrunken,
her skin loose, brittle as burned grass.
She rubs her eyes, looks around,
remembers who she was,
asleep for ages, wearied by dreams,
and slowly begins to rise.
Was she dead, is she now
returned to the earth?
Her hair outlined against clouds,
she throws a twig to the wind
to see what it will tell her.
The breeze flies away like a bird.
A strange new place, she thinks,
the land is dry, her tongue is dry,
making quick, excited clicks.
The low brown skyline has
scattered spines of bristled earth,
porcupine quills poking the sky,
rattling in the wind, a straggle
of white tree limbs, bleached bones
glinting in silence, the earth
hard, dark veins jutting
through aged flesh.
Has the land become the moon
she wonders? Made itself hollow
to take this dried up world with it?

It is early, the morning's soft flesh
forms on the horizon, warms

the parched earth as she
makes her way to the water hole
with an antelope,
she and the horned ones
both inheritors of water, not land.
She sits, is afraid, picks up
on the wind's refrain,
her heart a trembling echo.
She sings of the broken thread,
waits for a message to float
into her ear, turns the heels
of her feet in the direction
where she feels it might blow,
putting her ear to earth
to understand new sounds
as finely plucked as hunting bows.
The tired ground whispers,
sends voices, the sigh of plants,
the dark wailing of animals.
She hears the wild olive complaining
to the earth: *Too sandy, too loamy,*
too dry, I can't get my grip.
My fruit has become
dried black berries.

She hears morning mist complaining
to the wind: *Lift me, lift me up*
a wide fishnet of drops.
Take me on your light elbow,
let me drift, soft, over the spiky aloe.

Then the stream complains to the rock:
Just a trickle now, I streamed from high
kloof and valley to plateau and seashore;
a quick shift of your underbelly
and I slipped underground.

Poking the earth with a digging stick
she remembers that a certain tree
has a root that can be used as medicine
for curing the coughing of blood,
and tugging at another, recalls
it is the 'lucky plant' you burn
for ash to smear on your face,
so every man will love you.

Closing her eyes, the Bushwoman
waits quietly for a message,
threads in the sky to be climbed,
cobwebs or the hands of ancestors
that will help her along the way.
She makes a fire by rubbing twigs,
wrapping smoke in a blanket of grass,
blowing into it to bring ancestors,
inviting them to speak.

Her grass Bushman ancestor,
his face golden in the morning light,
speaks to her: *The stars fall*
when we die. When our hearts fall
over, we are not dead

but in a deep trance, lying
tightly strung like beads
from ostrich eggs,
bound together on a string.

She sits on her haunches, longing
for the taste of springbok,
wild honey, to feel cool water.
She adjusts the hide around her waist,
remembers when the desert lion
dragged a sleeping woman close
to the waterhole so he could drink
before he ate her, thinks of the numb
terror as the lion licked her tears.
This is how she feels.

NOTES

p 34
'Our Alignment'
Middens are ancient refuse heaps used for domestic waste such as mollusc shells, animal bones etc.

p 37
'Postcard from Another Era'
Ik heb jou lief is Dutch for 'I love you'.

pp 53 – 56
'When the Land Becomes the Moon'
This poem was inspired by writings from Janette Deacon and Craig Foster's: *My Heart Stands in the Hill*, which was originally sourced from records held in the Bleek and Lloyd Archive at the University of Cape Town.

p 55
'When the Land Becomes the Moon'
Kloof is a steep-sided ravine or valley.

ACKNOWLEDGEMENTS

Versions of the poems here collected first appeared
in the following magazines:

'Caracal' in *Stanzas*, 'Our Alignment' in *The Amsterdam
Quarterly*, 'The Migrant' in *New Contrast*, 'When the Land
Becomes the Moon' in *The Other Side of Sleep Anthology*,
'Sleeping with Morpheus', 'Lovebirds at the Pain Clinic', 'The
Home Bringing' in the *McGregor Poetry Festival 2016
Anthology*, 'Homing Pigeons', 'Messages from the Bees', 'The
Poet Who Talks to Birds' in *Off the Wall Anthology 2017*.

I am grateful to Douglas Reid Skinner for his advice.

Printed in the United States
By Bookmasters